# Kids Can Help the
# ENVIRONMENT

by **Emily Raij**

Consultant: Lisa Joyslin, Inclusive Volunteerism Program
Manager, Minnesota Association for Volunteer Administration,
St. Paul, Minnesota

CAPSTONE PRESS
a capstone imprint

Capstone Captivate is published by Capstone Press, an imprint of Capstone.
1710 Roe Crest Drive
North Mankato, Minnesota 56003
www.capstonepub.com

**Library of Congress Cataloging-in-Publication Data is available on the Library of Congress website.**
ISBN 978-1-4966-8376-2 (library binding)
ISBN 978-1-4966-8782-1 (paperback)
ISBN 978-1-4966-8427-1 (ebook pdf)

Summary: Make the world a cleaner, healthier place to live! This book is full of ideas and projects readers can put into action to help the environment.

**Image Credits**
iStockphot: SDI Productions, back cover, 14, SolStock, 20–21; Pixabay: DavidZydd (stripe background), 1 and throughout, rsull (leaf), 12 (bottom), 15 (top), 16, 21; Shutterstock: Andrey Norenko, 12 (top), Arthur Villator, 7, Bogdan Sonjachnyj, 23, Daniele Cossu, 15 (bottom), David Pereiras, 10–11, Dmitriy Kuznetsov, 24, Dragon Images, 8, Fevziie, 29 (bottom), Hairem, 4, hedgehog94, cover, Katerina Morozova, 18–19, kpakook, 13, lomiso, 17, Monkey Business Images, 9, New Africa, 26–27, Steven Frame, 11, Studio 2, 25, Thinnapob Proongsak, 22, Tongra239, 6, wavebreakmedia, 5, 28, 29 (top)

**Editorial Credits**
Editor: Erika L. Shores; Designer: Sara Radka; Media Researcher: Svetlana Zhurkin; Production Specialist: Tori Abraham

All internet sites appearing in back matter were available and accurate when this book was sent to press.

Printed in the United States of America.
PA117

# TABLE OF CONTENTS

# Caring for Earth

Do you enjoy having a picnic on one of those perfect sunny days? Maybe you like watching movies inside on a rainy night. Weather changes all the time. We can enjoy different seasons and the weather they bring. Fresh air and water are some of Earth's greatest gifts.

» Pollution from cars is a big reason for climate change.

» People like to spend time outside during warm weather.

**Climate** is the weather in a place over a long period of time. Climate has always been changing too. But scientists now know people are causing the world's climate to change in a dangerous way. We burn coal, oil, and gasoline in our homes, cars, and factories. We throw away too much garbage. All of these actions put harmful gases into Earth's **atmosphere**.

You may have heard about how those bad gases affect our climate. They absorb heat from the sun. The layer of gases is getting too thick. Heat cannot escape. That causes hotter temperatures on land and in water. This climate change is causing more storms, floods, heat waves, droughts, and wildfires. Extreme weather affects our health and safety. It harms our air, water, and food supply.

» Wildfires burn trees and grasses.

» Because of climate change, hurricanes and other storms can be more severe.

What can we do in our everyday lives to fight climate change? Making small changes in our homes and towns can have a big difference in the world. We can help the environment and be good global citizens. Taking an active role in your community shows you care about Earth.

# What Can I Do?

What things do you care about? How do you like to help? Think about how you can use what you like doing to help the earth. You might find that your knack for crafting or cleaning up comes in handy for some projects. If you like to grow things, that skill will be useful too.

» You can use your crafting skills to care for the earth.

» If you like doing work outdoors, you can find ways to help the planet.

You may feel like you have to fix a problem. But you don't need to be the hero. You can be the helper. That means you do not need to solve the whole problem. And you do not need to solve it right away. You just need to be part of the effort and work with others.

Some groups run programs and raise money to help the planet. These **charities** often take care of immediate needs. These are things that need to happen right away. That could mean cleaning up trash from water and land. You can help a charity collect money. Or you can **volunteer** directly with a cleanup at a beach or park.

» A charity might set up a day to clean beaches.

Environmental **activists** try to change laws that lead to more **pollution** and waste. They try to pass laws that limit pollution from factories. Other laws might limit the use of plastic bags or bottles.

» Skipping a car ride to school helps reduce some air pollution.

# Service Projects

## USING LESS FOSSIL FUELS

Air pollution is caused by burning **fossil fuels**, such as coal and oil. Driving less and walking more can help keep the air clean. Start a monthly or even weekly walk-to-school day. This lowers gas use and pollution from cars. Students can roll to school on bikes or rollerblades. Give your idea to the principal. Then set a date. Make posters to let your school know about the event.

**HELPING FACT**
Make posters showing how to be safe during walk-to-school days. Teach about crossing at crosswalks and always looking left-right-left.

You can also ask teachers, the mayor, or the police chief to walk with students on the event days. Ask some parents to track how many kids walk and roll on bikes, rollerblades, scooters, or skateboards. Parents can also hand out small prizes.

## Green Team

Students at Driftwood Middle School in Hollywood, Florida, found ways to use less energy in each classroom. They started a green team that looked at energy data for the school. Then they did weekly energy checks in each classroom. They checked if lights were left on or if electronics were plugged in. The team showed how much energy was being used in the school. Members would then leave ideas for teachers on how to use less energy. Unplugging and turning off computers was one easy change.

» You could grow peppers in a school garden.

Trees and plants remove harmful gases from the atmosphere. If you have room at home, start a garden. If you are short on space, you can start a windowsill herb garden. Or pick a few potted plants. You could also get space at a local community garden. Growing your own food means you buy less at the store. That is less food that has to be brought to the store on a truck or ship. And that means less air pollution too.

Start a school garden if there is space. A teacher or parent will need to help. Each grade can take care of its own garden bed. A garden club can plant and weed after school. Students, teachers, and families will enjoy fresh fruits and vegetables.

## Taking Action

A group of kids from 10 states filed a lawsuit against the U.S. government to stop the use of fossil fuels. If the government knows fossil fuels cause climate change, these children say burning the fuel goes against their rights to a healthy future. Students have also taken a day off school to **protest** climate change. Teen activist Greta Thunberg spoke to world leaders to tell them they are not doing enough to protect the planet.

## REDUCING WASTE

Turn waste into something useful! You can turn food scraps and yard waste into food for plants by **composting**. Instead of throwing out food scraps, you can put them in a compost bin. The bin can be a wooden, plastic, or metal box or tub. It can be placed in your yard or on your deck. Start by putting shredded newspaper, printer paper, or cardboard inside the bin. Then add worms! They will do all the work. The worms eat the food, leaves, and grass you put in the bin. The waste worms let out is compost.

Compost feeds the soil. It can be added to soil to help plants grow. Composting can easily become part of your family's everyday life.

**HELPING FACT**

Vegetable peels, food scraps, spoiled food, coffee grounds, tea leaves, and eggshells can all be composted. No pet waste or kitty litter can go in a compost bin. Also avoid dairy and meat or bones, which smell and may invite wild animals and pests.

» Composting food waste keeps tons of trash out of landfills every year.

There are many ways to turn your trash into treasures. **Recycling** is great, but you can "upcycle" to keep even more waste out of your bins. Upcycling is finding interesting ways to reuse things you probably have around the house.

Hold an upcycled crafting night with friends. You can make gifts out of things like glass jars, fabric scraps, paper tubes, and bottle caps. You can even melt old crayons into new ones. Use cookie cutters to create fun crayon shapes. From old basketballs to paint cans, plenty of things can be turned into planters. Give your gifts for holidays and birthdays. Or sell them to raise money for a charity that helps the earth.

» You can turn boring toilet paper tubes into fun and creative gifts.

» Picking up trash at the beach keeps ocean animals safe.

## CLEANING UP

You can't prevent trash altogether, but you can clean it up! Is there a beach, lake, or park in your area that needs some extra care? Plan a cleanup day. You can ask friends and family to join you. Or it can be something you do with a scouting troop, community **service** group, or a sports team you play on. If you ask the city or county that oversees the park, they may give you trash bags and cleanup supplies.

Plastics are some of the most harmful pieces of trash. Animals in forests and oceans may eat these things and get sick or even die. Picking up trash keeps it out of animals' homes and mouths.

### HELPING FACT
Clean up your school lunches! Plastic can take up to 1,000 years to break down in landfills. Replace plastic spoons and forks with reusable ones. Switch out plastic wrap for wraps made of cloth or beeswax.

# What If I Want to Do More?

Activists work to change something they think is wrong, such as a law. They look for solutions to the deeper cause of a problem. For example, an environmental activist might protest a big company whose factories pollute the air. One solution could be asking lawmakers to pass clean energy laws. These laws would make companies switch to cleaner energy, such as wind or solar.

» Solar and wind energy are safer for the planet.

» Cloth bags are better for Earth because they can be used over and over again.

An environmental activist also finds ways for communities to create less waste. They might ask stores to stop using plastic shopping bags. Shoppers can bring their own bags. This would even save the stores money. If enough people learn about the problems and solutions, companies will have to change their actions.

You do not have to be loud to make your concerns heard. Call or write to lawmakers. Discuss laws that harm the environment. Suggest helpful changes and new laws to protect land, air, and water. Send a letter to the editor of your local newspaper. Ask a parent if you can post on social media. Pass out information at town meetings or events. Make and pass out protest signs. Attend a **rally** just to listen.

» Signs are one way people can share their concerns with others.

» Environmental activists want other people to know about issues facing the planet.

Activists make other people aware of an issue. They want to help others take action. Activism can be quiet or loud. And it can change things in your town or across the world.

# Do What You Can

The health of our planet affects people now and for years to come. But Earth cannot speak for itself.

We can speak up and be the voice for change. Whether you want to lower energy use at your school or turn waste into something useful, there is a project for you.

Find projects that make good use of your time and talent. Think of what you care about. Think of what you like to do. You can work on your own or with a group. Our planet is big, but no action is too small to help!

» Picking up trash in a park is one of the many ways to care for the planet.

# Other Ways to Get Involved

» Be a trash runner! Pick up garbage you see during a walk, bike ride, or park visit.

» Make reusable shopping bags out of old T-shirts or jeans. Keep them on hand for trips to the grocery store or library.

» Hold an information night letting neighbors know about composting and how they can start.

» Start a "green team" at your school to help collect recycling from classrooms so that it is ready for pickup.

» Talk to your school leaders about switching from plastic cafeteria trays to ones that can be recycled or even composted. There are also compostable forks and spoons. Schools create lots of waste, so this can really make a difference.

» Make a video explaining Earth-friendly shopping tips. For example, avoid buying single-serve items of bottled water and snacks. Buy one large bag of snacks instead, which uses less packaging. Refuse plastic bags at the store. Use your own or carry items

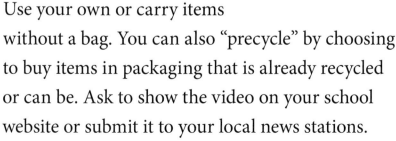

without a bag. You can also "precycle" by choosing to buy items in packaging that is already recycled or can be. Ask to show the video on your school website or submit it to your local news stations.

# Glossary

**activist** (AC-tiv-ist)—a person who works for social or political change

**atmosphere** (AT-muhss-fihr)—the mixture of gases that surrounds the earth

**charity** (CHAYR-uh-tee)—a group that raises money or collects goods to help those in need

**climate** (KLY-muht)—the average weather in a place over many years

**compost** (KOM-pohst)—to mix decaying leaves, vegetables, and other items so that they can be used in soil

**fossil fuel** (FAH-suhl FYOOL)—a natural fuel formed from the remains of plants and animals; coal, oil, and natural gas are fossil fuels

**pollution** (puh-LOO-shuhn)—harmful materials that damage the air, water, and soil

**protest** (pro-TEST)—to speak out about something strongly and publicly

**rally** (RAL-ee)—a large gathering of people with similar interests

**recycle** (ree-SYE-kuhl)—to make used items into new products; people can recycle items such as rubber, glass, plastic, and aluminum

**service** (SUR-viss)—a helpful or useful activity or action

**volunteer** (vol-uhn-TIHR)—to offer to do something without pay

# Read More

Gregory, Josh. *How to Compost at School.* New York: Smartbook Media Inc., 2018.

Shoals, James. *Recycling Works!* Broomall, PA: Mason Crest, 2020.

Wolny, Philip. *The Fight for the Environment.* New York: Rosen Publishing Group, 2020.

# Internet Sites

*ClimateKids*
climatekids.nasa.gov/how-to-help/

*Environmental Education for Kids*
www.eekwi.org/

*Reduce, Reuse, Recycle*
kids.niehs.nih.gov/topics/reduce/index.htm

# Index